PIONEERS OF SCIENCE

SAINT BENEDICT SCHOOL
DUFFIELD ROAD
DERBY DE22 1JD
Ti 3896

GALILEO

Douglas McTavish

Wayland

Pioneers of Science

Archimedes
Alexander Graham Bell
Karl Benz
Marie Curie
Thomas Edison
Albert Einstein
Michael Faraday
Galileo
Guglielmo Marconi
Isaac Newton
Louis Pasteur
Leonardo da Vinci

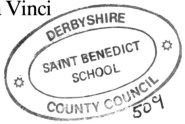

DERBYSHIRE
SAINT BENEDICT
SCHOOL
COUNTY COUNCIL
509

Book and series editor Rosemary Ashley
Designer David Armitage

First published in 1991 by
Wayland (Publishers) Ltd
61 Western Road, Hove
East Sussex BN3 1JD, England

© 1991 Copyright Wayland (Publishers) Ltd

British Library Cataloguing in Publication Data
McTavish, Douglas
    Galileo. – (Pioneers of Science)
    I. Title   II. Series
    500.81

    ISBN 0–7502–0163–0

Typeset by DP Press Ltd, Sevenoaks, Kent
Printed in Italy by Rotolito Lombardo S.p.A.
Bound in France by A.G.M.

Contents

DERBYSHIRE

SAINT BENEDICT
SCHOOL

COUNTY COUNCIL

1 ▼ Early Years

The house in Pisa, Italy, where Galileo was born in February 1564.

Galileo Galilei was born in Pisa, a city in the Italian republic of Florence, on 15 February 1564. He was the eldest of seven children. Not much is known about his brothers and sisters, although it is thought that three of them died when they were young. Galileo's father, Vincenzo, was a musician, and Galileo seems to have inherited from him a love of music; he learnt to play the lute at an early age and continued throughout his life. Galileo may have picked up another attribute from his father: an experimental approach to solving problems. Vincenzo examined the sounds made by vibrating musical strings, and set up experiments to test his theories. His son was later to study mathematics, physics and chemistry in a similar way.

As a child, Galileo was educated by a private tutor and he probably learned grammar, literature, arithmetic and geometry, the subjects usually taught at the time. When, in 1574, the family moved to Florence, Galileo attended a monastery school run by Jesuits. Vincenzo was determined that his son's education would enable him to earn a reasonable amount of money, and in 1581 he sent him off to Pisa University to study medicine.

The science that was taught in universities was based almost entirely on the teachings of the Greek philosophers – especially Aristotle – who had lived centuries earlier. Medicine was based on the work of Galen, who had died around AD 200. It was taken for granted that these scholars had examined all aspects of the world and explained its workings.

SAINT BENEDICT SCHOOL
DUFFIELD ROAD
DERBY DE22 1JD

This illustration, from the pages of a book published in 1508, depicts a flat Earth floating on water, with air and fire above. God is shown on Earth, creating Eve from Adam's rib.

The swinging pendulum

While listening to a sermon in Pisa cathedral in 1582, Galileo noticed a large chandelier swinging, like a pendulum, after it had been lit. He timed it with his pulse and noticed that, even though the swings became shorter as the chandelier slowed down, each complete swing took the same amount of time. From this observation he realized that the swings of a pendulum must be isochronal – that is, all its swings occurring at equal intervals. This discovery may have led him to invent what he called a pulsilogium, a device which used a pendulum to measure a patient's pulse rate.

However, Galileo was not the type of student who believed everything that was taught to him; in fact, he refused to accept anything that could not be proved by experiment. He questioned his tutors closely and, when their answers did not satisfy him, he did not hesitate to tell them so. Not surprisingly, he was not the most popular of students.

Galileo quickly lost interest in the study of medicine; it was too 'dry' and locked in the teachings of the past. Mathematics and physics excited him much more, and it was in these linked subjects that he is thought to have made his first independent discovery, concerned with the movement of a pendulum.

In 1585 Galileo left Pisa University and returned to Florence. He turned his attention to mathematics and shortly after began to give private lessons. He circulated two scientific manuscripts among his friends and started to gain a reputation in Florence as a mathematician. He hoped to gain a post as a professor of mathematics, either at Pisa or Siena, but no offers came. Galileo became increasingly impatient and in 1587 he decided to travel to Rome. He managed to get an introduction to Christopher Clavius, a famous Jesuit mathematician and astronomer, but little seems to have come from this meeting other than a lifelong friendship.

By now, despairing of finding work, Galileo returned once more to Florence. Eventually, in 1588, his growing reputation began to bring results and he was invited to give a series of lectures to the Academy of Florence. These lectures were a great success and this renewed his confidence. He was also fortunate in having as a friend and patron the Marquis Guidobaldo del Monte of Pesaro, who tried to use his influence on Galileo's behalf. He approached the universities at Padua and Bologna, but neither accepted Galileo.

FLORENTIA.

Then, in 1589, Guidobaldo was successful, and Galileo was appointed Professor of Mathematics at his old university, Pisa. He had been outspoken as a student, and it was not long before the university authorities discovered that Galileo's independent nature had not changed.

The city of Florence as it was during Galileo's time.

2 Ancient Wisdom

As we have seen, in the sixteenth century most of the accepted wisdom in science, medicine and mathematics was founded on the works of the Ancient Greeks. By about 300 BC, much of their knowledge had been gathered together in the famous Library at Alexandria, in Egypt. The finest scholars in the world visited the Alexandrian Library, and were encouraged to research and add to its store of knowledge. This store was already immense – by AD 200 the Library may have held as many as half a million works, but we shall never know for sure as it was completely destroyed by Muslim invaders in the seventh century.

The Alexandrian Library in Egypt contained thousands of manuscripts, and was visited by scholars from all over the ancient world.

Fortunately, not all Greek learning was lost. About two hundred years earlier, when a previous attack on the Library was anticipated, some scholars escaped and took important manuscripts with them. They settled in Byzantium (later known as Constantinople), and were soon followed by others. In time, however, the scholars were driven out of Constantinople, again taking original Greek manuscripts with them. Many went to Jundishapur in Persia, where study continued uninterrupted for two centuries. When Baghdad became the capital of the Muslim empire, the manuscripts were moved there, and the city became a famous centre of learning. Many Greek manuscripts were translated into Arabic, which became the accepted language for scientific and medical works.

Following the destruction of the Alexandrian Library, some scholars escaped to Byzantium, taking precious manuscripts with them.

The Muslim empire spread throughout the Middle East and North Africa, and even much of Spain was conquered. The turning point came when King Alphonso VI and the champion warrior El Cid drove the Muslims from central Spain and, in the process, freed the city of Toledo. Quite suddenly, the knowledge of the Greeks, guarded for so long by the Muslims, was available to western scholars.

When the crusaders recaptured parts of the Holy Land, they too returned with quantities of manuscripts. Throughout the twelfth and thirteenth centuries many Arabic documents were translated into Latin. They covered a vast range of learning, particularly in the sciences – including detailed works by Archimedes, Aristotle, Ptolemy

The ancient Greek philosopher Aristotle. During his lifetime (384–322 BC) he studied and wrote about a vast range of subjects, including physics, chemistry, biology, astronomy, cosmology, geology, politics and poetry.

An early printing press. Many people became familiar with the works of the ancient philosophers thanks to the spread of printed books.

and Hippocrates. Most of the translators were churchmen, and as they did their job they removed elements of Islamic bias that had been added by the Muslims, and even adjusted the texts to make them agree more closely with the teachings of the Christian Church. As a result, the ancient wisdom became the only acceptable, orthodox view of the world; to argue against it was to deny the authority of the Church and of God himself. The works of the Greek thinker Aristotle were particularly admired. He had lived from 384 to 322 BC, and had brought together all the knowledge of his own civilization and that of earlier ones. He had written

on a huge range of subjects, including what today we call biology, physics, chemistry, astronomy, geology, politics and much more. He seemed to have observed and explained almost everything.

At first the spread of classical learning was slow, as each manuscript had to be copied by hand. But, from the mid-fifteenth century, the printing press and the availability of printed books brought great changes. More and more people became familiar with the works of the Greeks and Romans, and came to respect what seemed to them to have been a golden age. The works printed were not those of Aristotle alone; the ideas of other philosophers and scientists, some of whom disagreed with Aristotle, were also published. Books of classical literature and poetry also appeared and were read eagerly.

This rebirth, or Renaissance, of classical knowledge first took root in Italy, where an atmosphere of intellectual curiosity and questioning grew. Old, accepted ideas were re-examined and new ones discussed openly. It was not long before the ideas of Aristotle came under fire. However, scholars did not suddenly abandon the beliefs that had been accepted for centuries; they simply came to realize that there might be a new way of looking at things.

This freedom of thought was to be rudely interrupted. In 1520, Martin Luther broke with the Catholic Church and set in motion the Protestant Reformation, a rebellion against the corruption and commercialism of the Church of Rome. As Luther's Protestant ideas began to gain ground in Italy in the 1530s and 1540s, the Church decided to suppress what it regarded as heresy. The Inquisition, with its powers of arrest, torture and execution, was strengthened. Any challenge to the Church and its teachings was to be dealt with ruthlessly.

Martin Luther, who began the Protestant Reformation.

The Universe as it was thought to be by Claudius Ptolemy, an astronomer who lived during the second century AD. Like Aristotle, Ptolemy placed the Earth at the centre, with the other three pure elements – water, air and fire – surrounding it. Beyond them were the planets, including the Sun, and the stars.

On returning to Pisa University, Galileo did not take long to make enemies among his Aristotelian colleagues. The first clash between them concerned the way in which bodies fall. The Greeks had believed that everything on Earth was made of a mixture of four pure elements – earth, air, fire and water.

Aristotle had noticed that these elements seemed to move in particular directions – the heavier ones, earth and water, fell downwards while the lighter ones, air and fire, moved upwards. He concluded that each element had its own 'natural' place, and the purpose of its movement was to reach that place. As he believed the Earth was at the centre of the Universe, it was 'natural' that all 'earthy' matter should fall towards the Earth, and that heavier bodies would fall faster.

14

Galileo disagreed with this theory. He stated that if two spheres of equal size, one of which is ten times as heavy as the other, are dropped, the heavier sphere does not fall ten times as fast as the lighter one. He probably carried out experiments to prove his point, and may even have demonstrated it publicly by dropping weights from the Leaning Tower of Pisa, although only his pupil, Vincenzo Viviani, described such an event. What Galileo certainly did, at least to his own satisfaction, was disprove Aristotle's claim.

The Leaning Tower of Pisa, from which Galileo is said to have dropped weights to demonstrate the rate of falling objects.

At that time, Galileo was writing a book about motion. In fact, he never published it, but writing it helped him to think through his ideas. Known as *On Motion*, the manuscript contains many attacks on Aristotle, especially his ideas about motion. Aristotle had identified two types of motion on Earth – the 'natural' motion of things trying to reach their natural place, and the 'forced' motion of objects that are moved by a living thing, such as a stone thrown by a person. In *On Motion*, Galileo argued that there was only one type of motion.

When Galileo's professorship at Pisa ended in 1592, he did not attempt to renew it. He returned to Florence and asked Guidobaldo del Monte to help him find another post. It was not long before Galileo was appointed Professor of Mathematics at Padua, a city in the Venetian Republic with a reputation for freedom of thought.

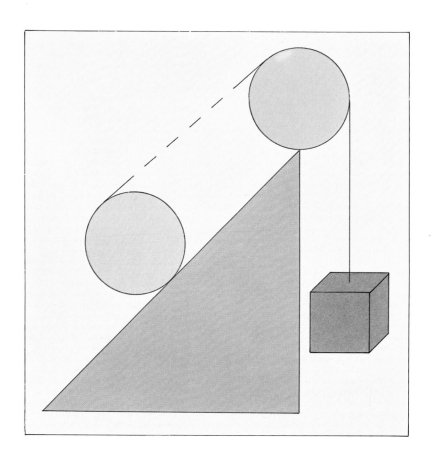

While he was Professor of Mathematics at Pisa, Galileo experimented with motion. This diagram is taken from an illustration in his notes describing his attempt to calculate the forces acting on spheres on different slopes.

An armillary sphere made in Florence in 1554. It was designed to show the paths of the planets orbiting the Earth.

He settled well in Padua and almost immediately made some influential friends. Although the university authorities at Padua were much more open-minded than those at Pisa, Galileo was still expected to teach a course that was largely based on Aristotle. To help his students to counteract this, he wrote a series of short papers for them. One such paper, known as *Mechanics*, dealt with the motion of objects rolling down inclined planes. Perhaps its most important conclusion was that a body on a horizontal plane needs only a small force to move it. In realizing this, Galileo had hit upon the principle of inertia, which was not to be fully described until Isaac Newton put forward his First Law of Motion about fifty years later.

Even though Galileo was earning three times as much as he had at Pisa, he decided to increase his income by setting up a workshop and making scientific instruments. This turned out to be a

Galileo's thermoscope. This was a simple type of thermometer which worked on the principle that air expands as it is heated. It had a graduated scale from which the temperature could be read.

profitable venture and one instrument, a geometrical and military compass, proved especially popular. Galileo did not invent the device, but in making improvements to it he completely redesigned it. By the time he had finished, his compass could be used to calculate multiplication and division, squares and square roots of numbers, and the density of metals and stones, as well as being useful in gunnery, surveying and navigation. It was, effectively, a combination of a portable calculator and a quadrant. As demand for the compass grew, Galileo had to appoint an assistant, and he claimed that the workshop eventually produced over three hundred compasses.

While at Padua he also looked into other areas of science, including heat and magnetism. He managed to produce magnets of great strength but his interest in magnetism was soon diverted by a much more exciting subject.

4 The Telescope

We do not know exactly how the telescope first reached Italy. It was invented in the Netherlands in 1608 and Galileo first heard of it the following year. He managed to get a description of the instrument and immediately constructed his own. He was then shown an example that had been offered to the Senate of Venice for a very high price; it was not even as good as his hastily constructed experimental telescope, and he advised the Senate not to buy it. Instead, he produced a far better version. On 21 August 1609, Galileo led the Senate to the top of a church tower to try out his new telescope. They were extremely impressed and,

Two of the telescopes built by Galileo between 1609 and 1610.

Above *In 1609 Galileo demonstrated his telescope to the Doge of Venice.*

when Galileo presented it to the Doge of Venice, he was immediately elected to the position of Professor of Mathematics at Padua for life, with a very high salary.

Galileo continued to make improvements to his telescope. The one he had given to the Doge was able to magnify nine times, but he soon built one with a magnification of thirty times. It was with this telescope that he was to make his most amazing discoveries and, in the process, embark on the road to his own downfall.

Until that time Galileo had not shown much interest in astronomy. He no longer accepted Aristotle's view that the Earth was at the centre of the Universe and the Sun and planets revolved around it. Galileo had heard the theories of Nicolaus Copernicus, that it was the Sun that occupied the central position and, although he privately thought that Copernicus was right, he was not totally convinced because there was no proof. Towards the end of 1609, Galileo turned his telescope on the night sky and gained all the proof he needed.

The Earth-centred Universe

In Galileo's time, it was taken for granted that the Earth was at the centre of the Universe. Aristotle had described the basic form of the Universe, stating that the Sun, Moon and planets all moved around the Earth in perfect orbits. Everything on Earth, below the Moon, was made up of the four pure elements, while the Moon and planets further from the Earth were all perfect spheres made of a fifth element called ether. The astronomer Ptolemy, who lived in the second century AD, modified Aristotle's idea, but still maintained that the Earth was at the centre.

To most people, this made good sense. Every day we see the Sun rise in the east and set in the west, therefore it must be moving around the Earth. What is more, if it were the Earth that moved instead of the Sun, everything on Earth that was not fixed in place would surely fly off into space.

In 1543 Copernicus published his claim that the Universe was heliocentric, or Sun-centred, but he had no real basis for this claim other than the fact it simplified Ptolemy's rather complicated calculations of the planets' orbits.

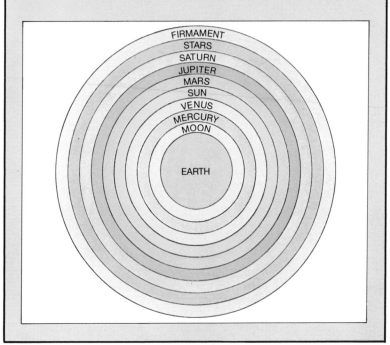

Opposite *The astronomer Nicolaus Copernicus (1473–1543) believed that the Sun was at the centre of the Universe and that all the planets, including the Earth, orbited around it.*

What Galileo saw through his telescope astonished and delighted him. He observed that the Moon was not the perfect, spherical body described by Aristotle; its surface was rough and covered with indentations and mountains. When he looked at Jupiter he saw that the planet had four moons of its own and was therefore a centre of motion, which demolished Aristotle's claim that only the Earth had such 'attendants'. Galileo also noticed countless stars never seen before.

Not surprisingly, he could not keep these discoveries to himself. Aristotle was wrong and Copernicus right, and Galileo wanted the world to

Below (left) Galileo's drawing of the crescent Moon. (Right) His drawing showing the Moon at the first quarter.

The imperfect Moon

Galileo wrote: 'It is a most beautiful and delightful sight to behold the body of the Moon . . . [It] certainly does not possess a smooth and polished surface, but one rough and uneven, and, just like the face of the Earth itself, is everywhere full of vast protuberances, deep chasms, and sinuosities.' He made his own drawings of the phases of the Moon, and showed its craters and plains. It was obvious to him that the Moon was definitely not the perfect sphere described by Aristotle.

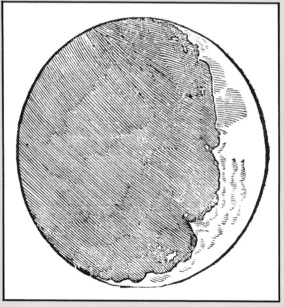
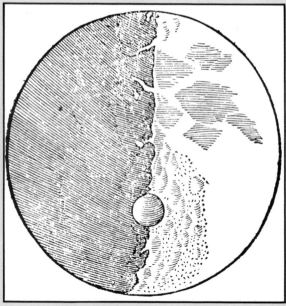

Two views of the Moon as seen from the Earth through a modern telescope.

know about it. In March 1610 he published *The Starry Messenger*; it caused a sensation and was an immediate best-seller. The Aristotelians and many sections of the Catholic Church were outraged.

In September Galileo left the relative safety of Padua and the protection of the Venetian state, and returned to Florence. This was not a wise move, but he had always wanted recognition at the court of the Medicis, the powerful ruling family of Florence. His discoveries had gained him this recognition, and he had been made 'Philosopher and Mathematician to the Grand-Duke', Cosimo de' Medici. At last Galileo felt he was on firm ground, and that all he had to do was demonstrate that Copernicus was right and everybody would listen. He realized later how wrong he was, but by then it was too late.

5 ▽ The Storm Clouds Gather

Galileo points out to Cosimo de' Medici the moons of Jupiter which he discovered in 1609.

Galileo continued his telescope observations in Florence. He spotted that Saturn seemed to have two stars beside it; they were in fact what we now know to be Saturn's rings, but Galileo's telescope was not powerful enough to show this. Far more importantly he noticed that, like the Moon, Venus had phases and seemed to change in size. This could only mean that it moved around the Sun and not around the Earth.

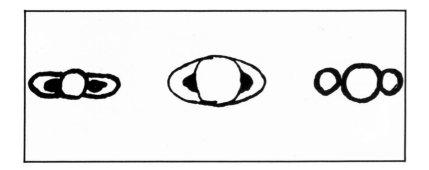

Left *Galileo's sketch of Saturn showing what he believed to be two other bodies orbiting the planet.*

The Aristotelian were dismayed. If Galileo's observations were correct they would have to abandon their view of the Universe. They decided to defend their belief by saying that what Galileo had seen through his telescope were mere optical illusions. Some even refused to look through a telescope themselves.

Below *If Galileo's telescope had been more powerful, he would have realized that Saturn was encircled by rings.*

The German astronomer Johannes Kepler (1571–1630) supported Galileo's claim that the Copernican view of the Universe was correct, but he was too far away to help Galileo convince his critics.

To strengthen his case, Galileo sought confirmation of his observations from an independent source. The astronomer Johannes Kepler had already given his backing, but he was a long way away in Prague. Galileo felt his best chance was to visit Christopher Clavius at the Jesuit College in Rome. This he did in March 1611. Clavius and his fellow astronomers looked through the telescope that Galileo had brought, and saw for themselves what he had described. They congratulated him for his invention but they did not admit that what they had seen was evidence of a heliocentric Universe. The Church had appointed a special commission, headed by Cardinal Bellarmine, to examine Galileo's discoveries. When Clavius reported to the Cardinal he told him they contained nothing to prove that Copernicus was right.

Galileo, meanwhile, went to visit Cardinal Maffeo Barberini, himself a mathematician but also a rich patron of science and the arts. Galileo thought that Barberini agreed with his views of the Universe, but understood that he could not be persuaded to admit it publicly, at least for the time being. Galileo was also seen by Pope Paul V, and it appears that he made a good impression. Finally, in June, he went home to Florence convinced that his visit had been a total success.

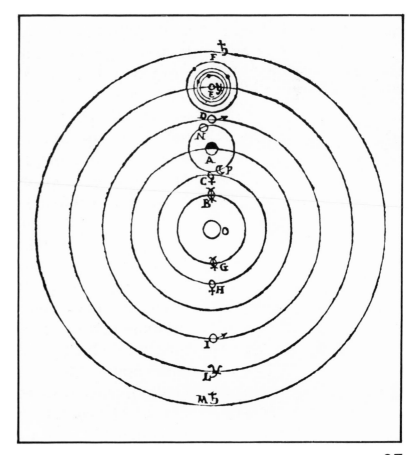

Galileo's own drawing of the Copernican Universe, showing the four moons of Jupiter.

He was unaware that his enemies were gathering their forces. They included professors with whom he had clashed during his time at Pisa, other Aristotelian scholars, and people in Florence who were jealous of his position at court. Led by a leading scholar, Ludovico delle Colombe, they began their attacks in Florence. They quoted Aristotle's explanation that some things float on water because of their shape rather than because of what they are made of, knowing that Galileo would not be able to restrain himself from arguing. The dispute started quietly and privately, but it soon became public. In the end, Galileo accused delle Colombe of being unable to understand what he was talking about.

At about the same time Galileo started another dispute, with Father Christoph Scheiner, a Jesuit astronomer. Scheiner had looked through his own telescope and seen that the surface of the Sun appeared to be marked with spots. He concluded that the spots were, in fact, small planets orbiting close to the Sun and that there were probably many others like them orbiting Jupiter. Galileo took this as a criticism of his own observations, and did not believe that the Sun's 'spots' were planets at all. He wrote a series of letters refuting Scheiner and presenting his own evidence. When these letters were published they made it plain to everyone that Galileo was determined in his support of the Copernican Universe.

Delle Colombe now went on to the attack again, this time concentrating on the religious implications of Galileo's work. He began to spread rumours that Galileo had denied the authority of the Bible, which clearly stated that the Earth stood still. Some churchmen, already suspicious of Galileo, started to voice their suspicions loudly. On 20 December 1614, a Dominican preacher named Tommaso Caccini gave a sermon that

Through his telescope, Galileo saw that the surface of the Sun was marked with spots. These sunspots had also been observed by the Jesuit astronomer Christoph Scheiner, who believed they were small planets circling the Sun.

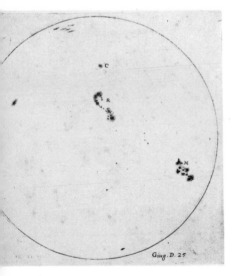

Cardinal Roberto Bellarmine (1542–1621) probably began collecting evidence against Galileo as early as 1611.

openly attacked mathematics as the work of the devil, and denounced Copernicus and Galileo as heretics. News of the sermon eventually reached the Inquisition in Rome. At last, Galileo realized that powerful forces were at work, and for the first time he was seriously concerned.

Cardinal Bellarmine, a strong upholder of the Church's teachings, challenged Galileo to deny that his view of the Universe contradicted the Bible. Galileo tried to do so, but he was a scientist not a theologian, and his answer was not entirely to Bellarmine's liking. Galileo again decided to go to Rome and plead his case. He was unable to see any of the influential figures he hoped to win over, and found himself being drawn into arguments on all sides. He eventually managed to clear himself of the accusation of heresy, but was unable to prevent the Church from declaring that Copernicus' view of the Universe went against the Scriptures.

This was bad enough, but worse was to come. In 1616 the Pope told Bellarmine to summon Galileo and order him not to 'hold or defend' the Copernican view. Galileo realized that he had no option but to agree. He comforted himself with the thought that at least he had survived to fight again and might be able to bring up the subject of the Sun-centred Universe in the future.

Galileo's enemies also believed that his silence would be short-lived, and they were determined to catch him out when next he revealed his Copernicanism. They placed in the Vatican records a forged document. This was a false account of Galileo's meeting with Bellarmine which stated that he had been ordered not to hold or defend the opinion that the Sun was at the centre of the Universe, *nor teach it in any way*.

Galileo, of course, knew nothing of this. Back in Florence he gave every impression of having learnt his lesson. He returned to the safer study of lenses and optics and did his best to steer clear of controversy. Trouble, however, had a way of finding him.

During 1618, three bright comets appeared in the sky. They caused a great deal of speculation and a number of pamphlets were published about them. One such pamphlet was produced by the Jesuit College in Rome, and rumours reached Galileo that it contained proof that Copernicus was wrong. In fact, it did not mention Copernicus, as Galileo found when he read the pamphlet for himself. However, he could not resist the temptation to ridicule it. He published his response, entitled *Discourse on the Comets*, under the name of one of his pupils, but this fooled no one. Incensed, the Jesuits attacked again, and again Galileo responded. In 1623 he published *The Assayer*. The book poked fun at the Jesuit College and the Jesuits were far from pleased.

Left *Galileo noting down his observations in his study outside Florence.*

31

Two months before *The Assayer* appeared, a new pope was installed in the Vatican. Known officially as Pope Urban VIII, he was in fact none other than Galileo's friend Maffeo Barberini. In April 1624 Galileo visited him in Rome, convinced that he would be able to persuade the Pope to permit discussion of the Copernican theory. Urban agreed, but insisted that Galileo must present a balanced account of the two world systems and not come out in favour of the heliocentric view. Galileo knew that Urban would go no further, and back in Florence he began work.

We shall never know how hard Galileo tried to make his account balanced and impartial. We do know that he failed. When it appeared in 1632, the

In 1623, Galileo's friend Maffeo Barberini became Pope Urban VIII.

An illustration from the first edition of Galileo's Dialogue on the Two Great World Systems, *published in 1632. The three figures are Aristotle, Ptolemy and Copernicus.*

Dialogue on the Two Great World Systems sold out. The book was written in Italian rather than Latin, and so many more people were able to read it. What is more, it was not a dry scientific work, but presented in the form of a lively discussion between three friends, Sagredo, Salviati and Simplicius. The last of these, Simplicius, was portrayed as a rather foolish Aristotelian philosopher who was frequently ridiculed by the Copernican Salviati and unable to convince the third, 'impartial' friend, Sagredo, of the truth of his arguments.

Galileo's enemies saw their chance. The Jesuits complained to Pope Urban that the *Dialogue* was biased in favour of Copernicus, and hinted that the character Simplicius represented the Pope. Urban was enraged. He appointed a commission of enquiry and, when it reported that what the Jesuits had said was true, Galileo's book was withdrawn. In September 1632 Urban gave the order: 'His Holiness charges the Inquisitor at Florence to inform Galileo, in the name of the Holy Office, that he is to appear as soon as possible in the course of the month of October at Rome before the Commissary-General of the Holy Office.'

The court of the Inquisition in Rome. Galileo was tried by the court in 1633.

Galileo was in a state of shock. He could not believe that his friend had handed him over to the Inquisition. When he realized that he had no other choice, he set out for Rome in the middle of January, 1633. It was several weeks before the Inquisition called him to trial, and by that time Galileo had convinced himself that he had little to fear. After all, he had Cardinal Bellarmine's signed letter of 1616, forbidding him to 'hold or defend' the Copernican view, and he believed he had obeyed this instruction. He expected that he would have to defend his book and produce Bellarmine's letter, and he felt he was on firm ground.

However, the Inquisition was not like a court of law today; the accused was not given a copy of the charges against him, nor of the evidence, and he had no lawyers to represent him. When the trial moved on to the events of 1616 and Galileo's meeting with Cardinal Bellarmine, the judges triumphantly drew his attention to the forged document that forbade him to teach the Copernican doctrine in any way, either verbally or in writing. Galileo, naturally, was astounded. He did not remember the document, simply because it was a forgery that had been placed in the Vatican records by his enemies. He could not even ask Bellarmine to back him up; the Cardinal had died some years earlier.

After the hearing, Galileo was visited by the Commissary-General of the Inquisition, who told him that the proceedings could drag on for a long time. If Galileo refused to confess, the Inquisition had ways of persuading him – torture, for example – and could have him burned at the stake. His only hope of mercy was to admit his guilt, and the judges would not treat him harshly. Galileo agreed; he could not win against such powerful opposition and he knew that the threat of torture was not an idle one.

At the end of his trial, Galileo felt he had no choice but to confess his guilt and say that he had been mistaken in his belief that the Earth was at the centre of the Universe.

On 30 April Galileo appeared again before the Inquisition and confessed. He said that he had, mistakenly, presented the Copernican view in too favourable a light, and that he had been wrong to say that the Earth moved around the Sun. On 22 June the sentence was announced, and all Galileo's hopes of lenient treatment were dashed. He was to deny publicly that he believed the Copernican doctrine and was to be imprisoned for the rest of his life. The *Dialogue* and all of his other works were to be banned, and he must publish no more books.

Fortunately, the conditions of Galileo's imprisonment were not too severe. In December 1633 he was permitted to return to his own villa at Arcetri, outside Florence. He was allowed to write and receive letters, and he began working again.

As he was forbidden to write about Copernicus, he turned his attention back to the subjects of motion and mechanics. He drew together and clarified some of the principles he had first examined in his manuscript *On Motion*, especially the way in which bodies fall. He attempted to slow down the motion by rolling spheres down slopes, so that the speed and time they took to fall was

In 1638 Galileo was visited in prison by the English poet John Milton.

Although he was officially forbidden to publish his work, Galileo continued his studies during his later life.

easier to measure. In this way he was able to arrive at the precise relationships between the speed of a falling body, the distance it falls and the time it takes. Galileo always wrote out his conclusions in full, but when they are converted into modern algebraic form, his laws of free-fall are:

$$\text{distance} \, \alpha \, \text{time}^2$$
$$\text{velocity} \, \alpha \, \text{time}$$
$$\frac{\text{velocity} \, \alpha \, \text{time}}{2} = \text{distance}$$

where v is the velocity (speed), t is the time taken to fall, s is the distance fallen, and α means 'proportional to'. Scientifically speaking, these were some of the most important statements he ever made.

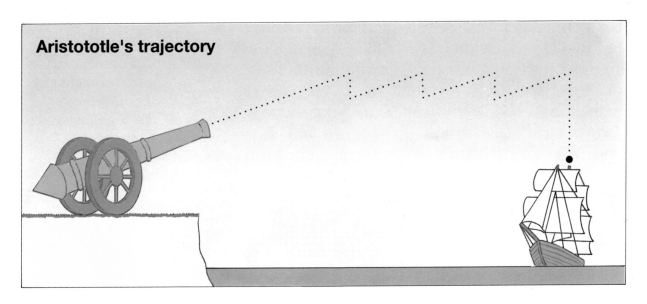

Aristototle's trajectory

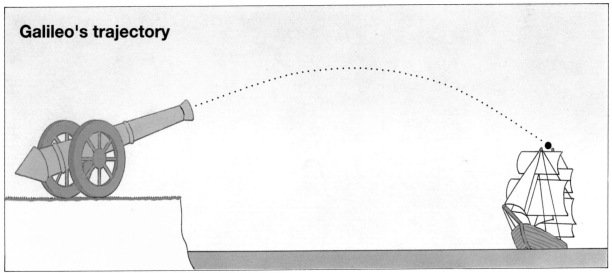

Galileo's trajectory

Aristotle believed the path of a projectile was the result of two separate types of motion, the forced motion which pushed it forward and the natural motion that caused it to fall to its proper place, the Earth (Top) Galileo disproved this and showed that projectiles and other bodies moved because of forces acting upon them. (Lower)

The type of motion that was most often studied in Galileo's time was to do with projectiles, because of its importance in gunnery and warfare. Using his laws of free-fall, Galileo was able to show that the path of a projectile, such as a cannon ball, was a parabola (a certain type of curve). In doing so, he disproved Aristotle's claim that the path of such bodies was a result of two types of motion, forced and natural, and showed that all bodies moved because they were acted upon by forces. He did not know what these forces were. For example, he thought that the planets might be held in orbit around the Sun by magnetism, and it was not until 1687 that Isaac Newton was able to explain that the force of attraction was, in fact, gravitation.

Galileo collected together these and other studies in a book he called *Discourses and Mathematical Demonstrations concerning Two New Sciences*. Because he was banned from

An illustration from Galileo's Discourses *showing how the breaking point of a beam depends upon the material, the thickness and the force exerted upon it.*

This 'composite' picture shows some of the planets of our Solar System, though not in their correct positions.

publishing his work, he passed the manuscript to a friend who smuggled it out of Italy to the Netherlands, where it was printed. Galileo was able to claim that he had no knowledge of the book's publication. Like his *Dialogue, Discourses* was written in Italian and was in the form of discussions between Sagredo, Salviati and Simplicius. All three 'friends' seem to have learned from the past, however, as Simplicius appears rather less stupid than he was in the *Dialogue*, and Sagredo and Salviati seem less determined to prove his foolishness.

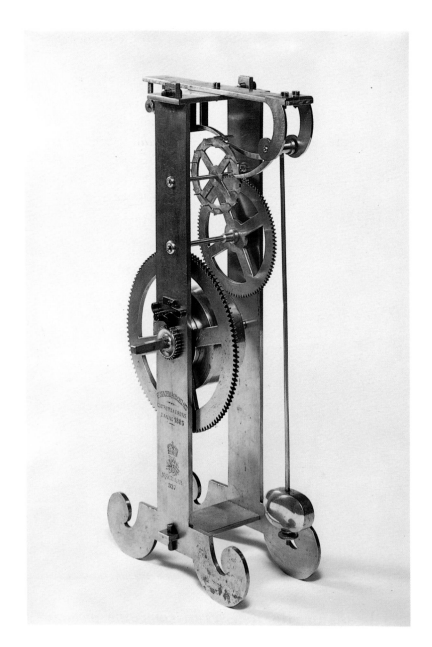

A model of a clock movement designed by Galileo in 1641, shortly before his death.

In 1636 and 1638 Galileo had two important visitors – the philosopher Thomas Hobbes and the poet John Milton. Shortly after, he began to have severe problems with his eyes and by 1639 he became totally blind. He was joined in Arcetri by two of his former pupils, Vincenzo Viviani and Evangelista Torricelli, who helped him to continue his work. In November 1641 he was confined to bed with a fever and a kidney complaint, and on 8 January 1642 he died.

Galileo's Legacy

Some of the instruments made by Galileo. On the left is his military compass and, on the right, two of his telescopes.

Just as Galileo's trial and confession marked the end of the Copernican doctrine in Italy, his death brought the end of an era. The spirit of scientific enquiry now passed from Italy to northern Europe, where freedom of thought was not restricted by the teachings of the Catholic Church. However, the fact that this spirit existed at all is largely thanks to Galileo.

Isaac Newton was born in 1642, the year of Galileo's death. His theory of gravitation finally laid to rest the idea of the Earth-centred Universe and showed that Galileo had been right.

The sheer breadth of his interests and knowledge are impressive, as was his ability to free himself of the accepted 'truths' of his time, to think the 'unthinkable'. Perhaps the most important thing about him was the way in which he worked. He was the first person to put into practice a truly scientific method; when he had an idea he built the equipment to test it experimentally, and then analysed the results. He rarely used the results of his experiments to prove his theories to others – they were more for his own satisfaction – but nonetheless his method of working became widely accepted.

Galileo was convinced that mathematics could be used to describe many aspects of the natural world. 'The book of the Universe', he wrote, 'is written in the language of mathematics.' He tried to tackle all problems by reducing them to considerations of mathematical quantities. such as weight, time, distance and speed, and scientists soon began to ignore Aristotle's four 'elements'.

His work was really only the beginning. Even before he died, his pupils were using his methods to break new ground themselves. Outside Italy, his influence was probably greatest in England, among the members of the Royal Society and, particularly, with Isaac Newton, whose theory of gravitation finally got rid of the idea of the Earth-centred Universe. The movement of the Earth, however, was not proved by experiment until the mid-nineteenth century. Galileo was eventually forgiven by the Roman Catholic Church, but not until 1979.

A statue of Galileo. He was one of the most remarkable of all pioneers of science.

Date Chart

1564 Galileo born in Pisa.

1581 Begins to study medicine at Pisa University.

1585 Leaves Pisa for Florence, where he teaches mathematics.

1589 Becomes Professor of Mathematics at Pisa University.

1590–91 May have carried out experiments on Leaning Tower of Pisa; wrote *On Motion*.

1592 Moves to Padua, as Professor of Mathematics.

1597 Designs military compass.

1602–09 Does his most important work on motion.

1609 Improves newly discovered telescope and begins astronomical observations.

1610 *The Starry Messenger* published; leaves Padua for Florence.

1611 Visits Rome where he demonstrates his telescope.

1614 Denounced in church sermon.

1616 Instructed by Church not to 'hold or defend' the Copernican view.

1618 Three comets appear, causing much speculation about the nature of the Universe.

1619 *Discourse on the Comets* published.

1623 *The Assayer* published. Maffeo Barberini becomes Pope Urban VIII, and gives Galileo permission to write book on rival cosmologies.

1623–31 Works on the *Dialogue on the Two Great World Systems*.

1632 The *Dialogue* published; Galileo summoned to Rome.

1633 Tried by Inquisition and sentenced to life imprisonment.

1638 *Discourses and Mathematical Demonstrations concerning Two New Sciences* published in the Netherlands.

1639 Becomes totally blind.

1642 Death.

SAINT BENEDICT SCHOOL
DUFFIELD ROAD
DERBY DE22 1JD

Books to Read

Discoveries and Opinions of Galileo by S. Drake (Doubleday, 1957)

Galileo by Colin Ronan (Weidenfeld and Nicolson, 1974)

Galileo and the Birth of Modern Science by Martin Suggett (Wayland, 1981)

Galileo at Work by S. Drake (University of Chicago Press, 1978)

Galileo Galilei: His Life and Works by R.J. Seeger (Pergamon, 1966)

Isaac Newton by Douglas McTavish (Wayland, 1990)

Spotlight on the Age of Scientific Discovery by L.W. Cowie (Wayland, 1987)

The Ascent of Man by Jacob Bronowski (BBC Publications, reprinted 1988)

Glossary

Aristotelians Followers of the ideas put forward by Aristotle (384–322 BC)

Astronomy The scientific study of the stars, the planets and space.

Body (in physics) Any physical object.

Classical Relating to the Ancient Greeks and Romans.

Copernican Relating to the theories of Nicolaus Copernicus (1473–1543).

Cosmology The study of the Universe.

Ether To Aristotle, the fifth natural element, thought to be purer than the other four.

Force The push or pull that makes something move, slows it down or stops it.

Geocentric With the Earth at the centre, as in Aristotle's view of the Universe.

Gravitation The force of attraction between any two objects in the Universe.

Heliocentric With the Sun at the centre, as in Copernicus' view of the Universe.

Heresy An opinion or belief that is contrary to the established beliefs of the Catholic Church.

Inertia It causes a body to remain at rest or, if it is moving, to continue in the same direction and in a straight line unless it is acted upon by a force.

Inquisition An institution of the Roman Catholic Church, which punished those who defied the Church's teachings.

Jesuit A member of the Society of Jesus, founded in 1534.

Lute A type of stringed musical instrument.

Matter The material that makes up a physical object.

Muslim A follower of the faith of Islam.

Optics The science relating to sight and the laws of light.

Orthodox Conforming to the Christian faith as established by the early Church.

Parabola A special type of curved shape.

Philosophy Literally, 'the love of wisdom'. It has come to mean the study of events and actions in terms of their causes and reasons.

Projectile An object that is thrown or fired through the air.

Quadrant An instrument used in astronomy and navigation for measuring the altitudes of stars.

Reformation A religious movement in the sixteenth century, originally intended to reform the Catholic Church. It eventually led to the founding of Protestant Churches.

Renaissance The period of European history between the Middle Ages and the modern world, which saw a revival of the study of Ancient Greece and Rome, and great artistic and scientific achievements.

Theology The study of God, his relation to humans and the universe, and of faith and the teachings of the Bible.

Vatican The palace of the popes in Rome.

Picture acknowledgements

The Ancient Art & Architecture Collection 10, 19, 45; Mary Evans 4, 8, 11, 15, 24, 26, 29, 30, 32, 34, 36, 37, 43; Michael Holford 17, 18, 42; The Mansell Collection 9; Ann Ronan Picture Library 5, 6, 14, 23 (both), 25 (lower), 27, 28, 33, 40; Science Photo Library 22 (both), 41; Wayland Picture Library iii, 12, 13, 20 (lower), 38, 44; ZEFA 25 (top). Artwork on pages 16, 21 and 39 is by Jenny Hughes. Cover artwork is by Richard Hook.

Index